Adaline

Name Writing Practice

Personalized Name Writing Activities for
Pre-schoolers to Kindergarteners

Visit Us At:

BeeSmarterBooks.com

Check our Search Engine for a child's name. We're
adding more personalized books often. Or use our
contact page to let us know the name you're
looking for.

Also, be sure to sign up for a mailing list to stay up
to date on our newest books & grab your free gift.

Dear Parent, Grandparent or Wonderful Friend,

First, thank you for buying this book for your child.

We've strived to create a book that will help you with the most important first skill a child can learn, identifying, learning and writing their own name.

The book if personalized for your child, with their name. There are 100 pages of fun activities and practice pages. Some pages are single activities to help build their skills. Many are practice pages. Some meant for developing the fine motor skills needed to starting writing. There are also lots of lined (ground, fence, sky) pages with your child's name ready to be traced.

As you child master the tracing skill, you'll find more lined pages to putt that skill to use with writing their without trace lines. The final skill in this book is writing without the lines, inside a box.

Please feel free to remove pages and use them as master copies to be duplicated as needed. We find an xacto knife or razor blade is the best way to remove these pages. (Be care, though).

We'd love to hear your feedback, so take a few moment if you can. Also, please stop our website, BeeSmarterBook.com. Sign up for our email list (we have more books for young learners on their way) and grab your free gift.

Thanks,

Katherine (aka BeeSmarter Mom)

This Is
My Book

Adaline

Writing Warm-Up 1

Directions: Trace the shapes in each row.

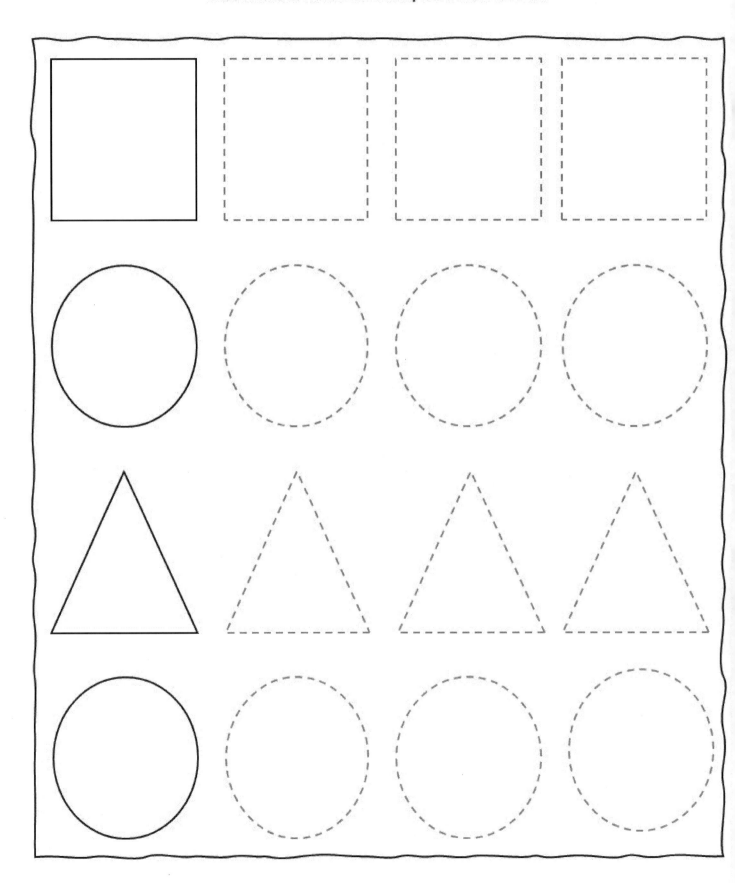

Writing Warm-Up 1

Directions: Trace the shapes in each row.

Writing Warm-Up 1

Directions: Trace the shapes in each row.

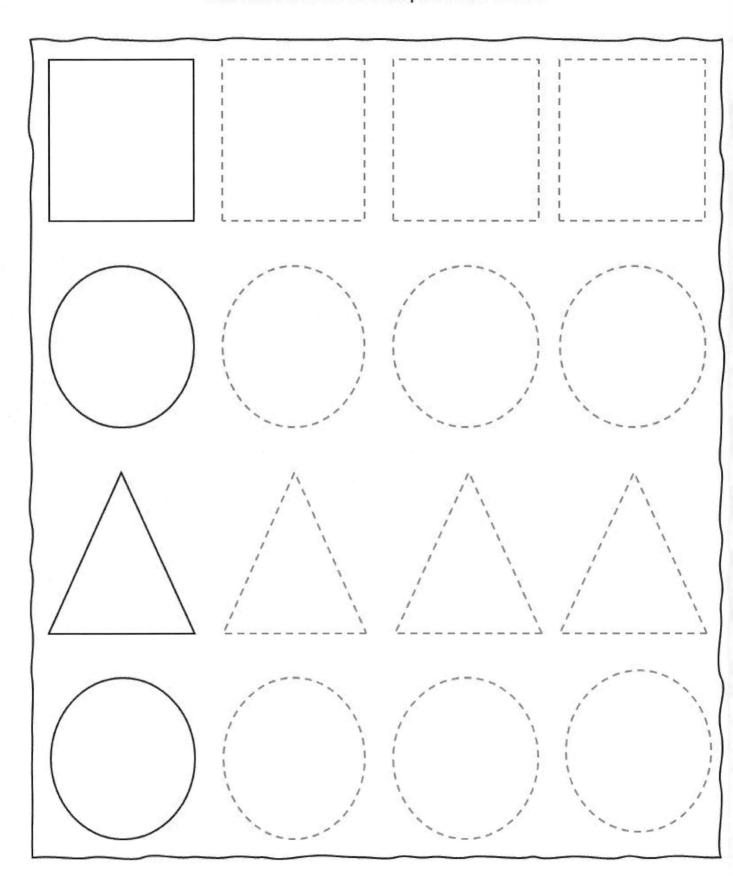

Writing Warm-Up 1

Directions: Trace the shapes in each row.

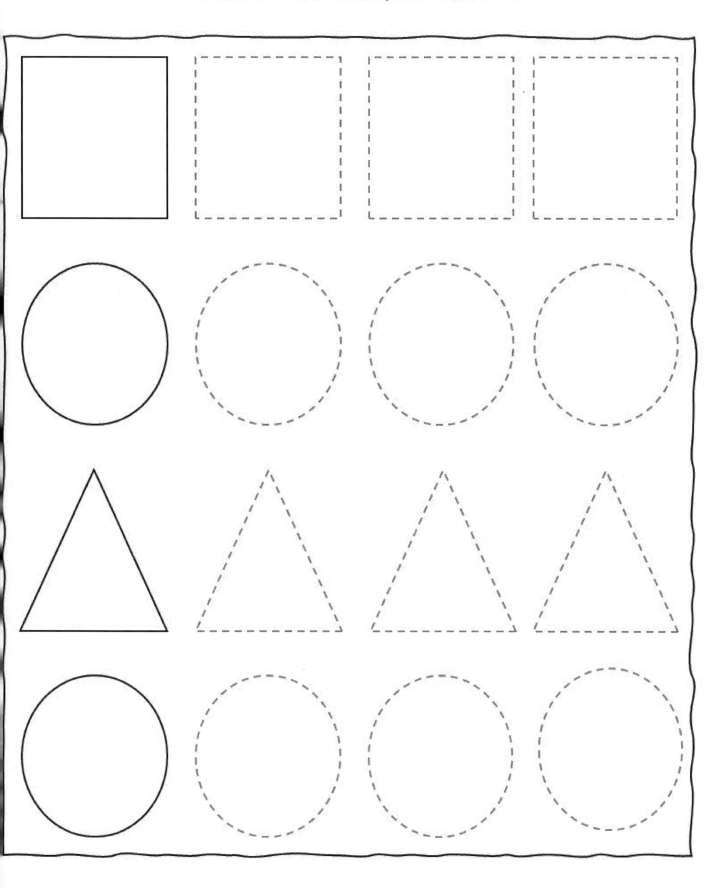

Writing Warm-Up 1

Directions: Trace the shapes in each row.

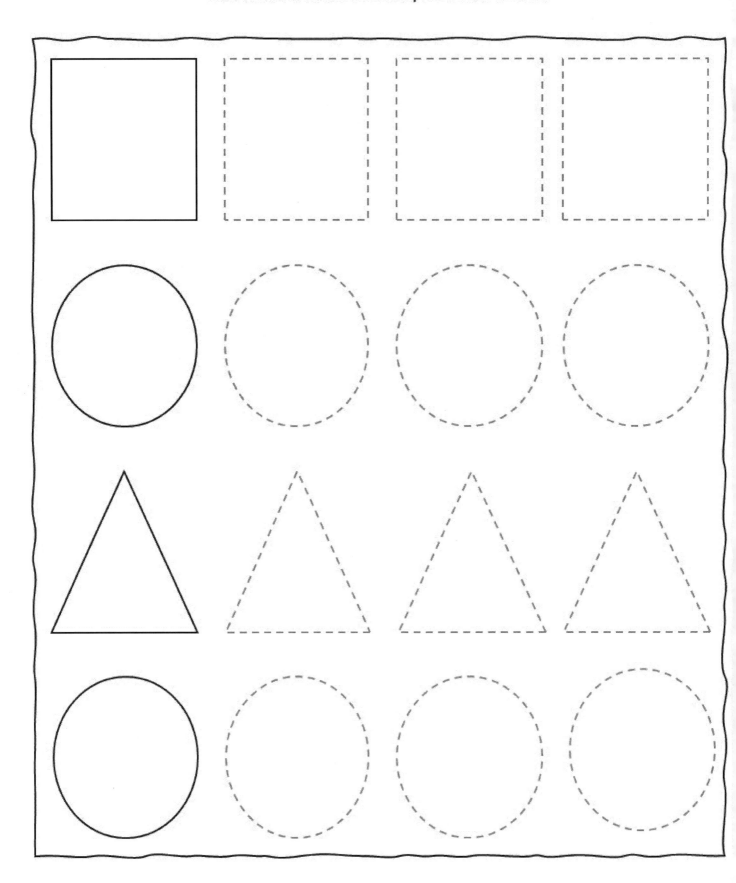

Writing Warm-Up 1

Directions: Trace the shapes in each row.

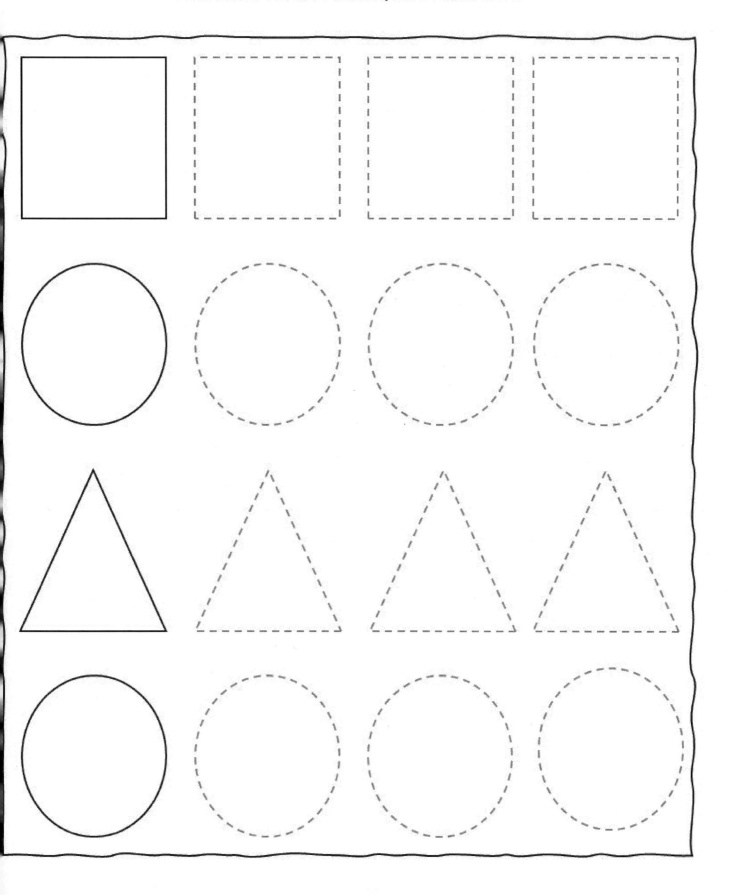

Writing Warm-Up 2

Directions: Trace the lines in each row.

Writing Warm-Up 2

Directions: Trace the lines in each row.

Writing Warm-Up 2

Directions: Trace the lines in each row.

Writing Warm-Up 2

Directions: Trace the lines in each row.

Writing Warm-Up 2

Directions: Trace the lines in each row.

Writing Warm-Up 2

Directions: Trace the lines in each row.

Writing Warm-Up 3

Directions: Trace around the balloons and the strings leading to the bow.

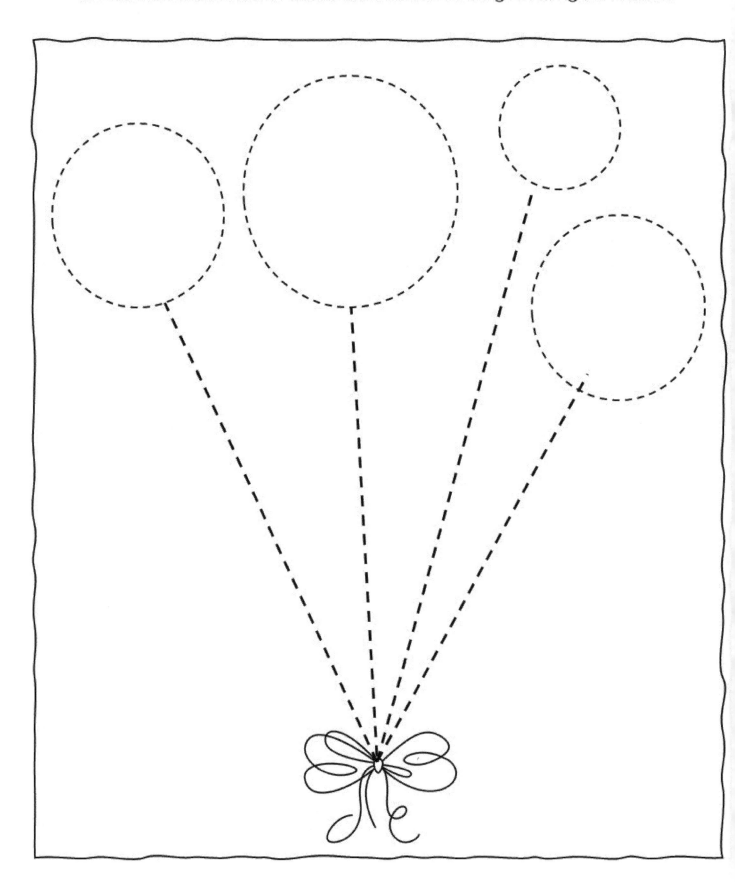

Writing Warm-Up 3

Directions: Trace around the balloons and the strings leading to the bow.

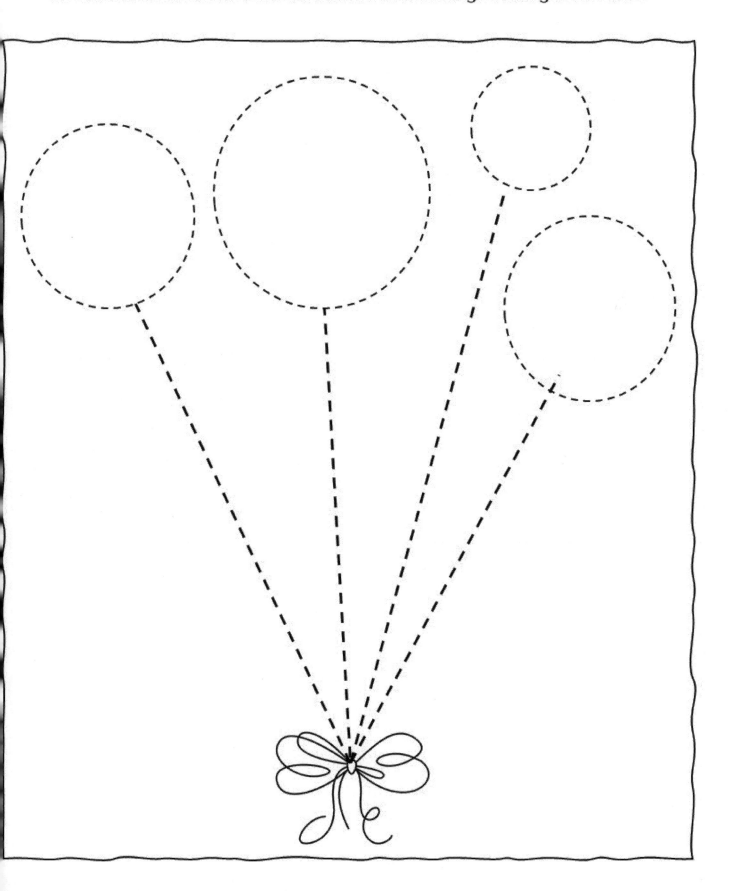

Writing Warm-Up 3

Directions: Trace around the balloons and the strings leading to the bow.

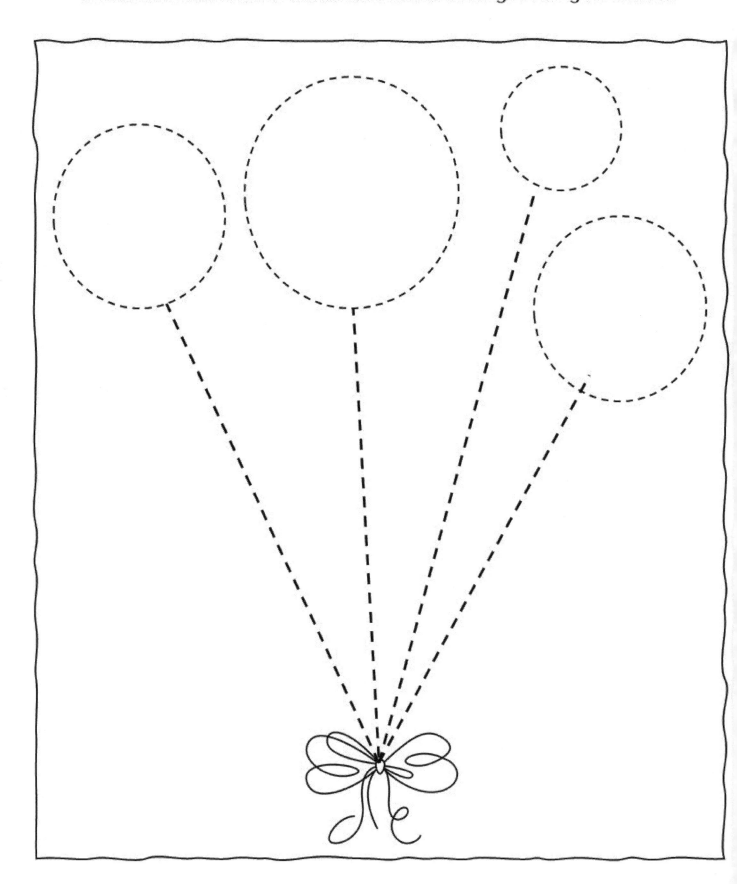

Writing Warm-Up 3

Directions: Trace around the balloons and the strings leading to the bow.

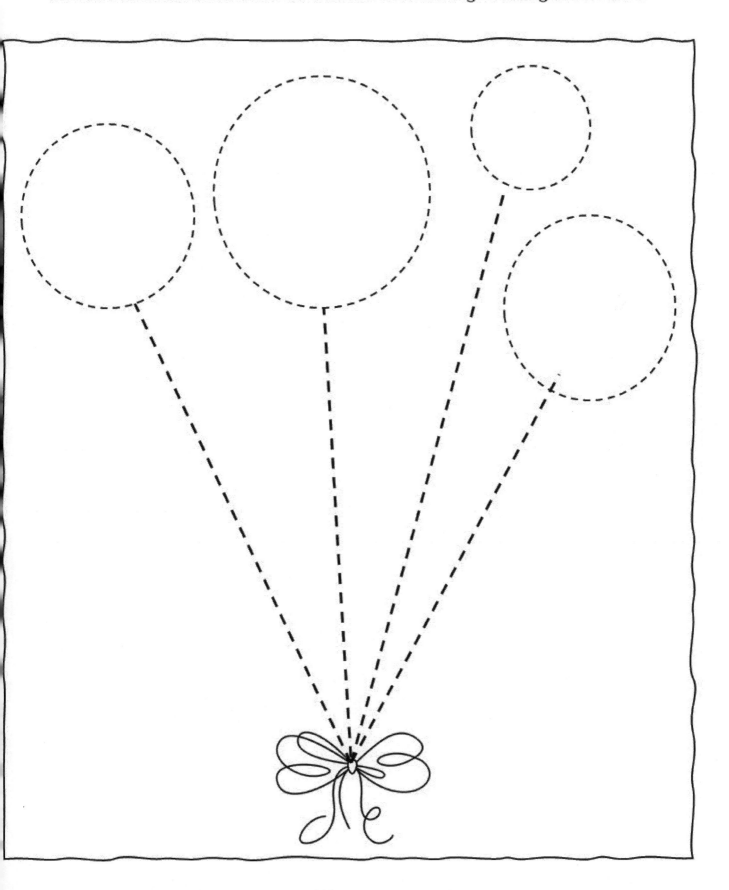

Writing Warm-Up 3

Directions: Trace around the balloons and the strings leading to the bow.

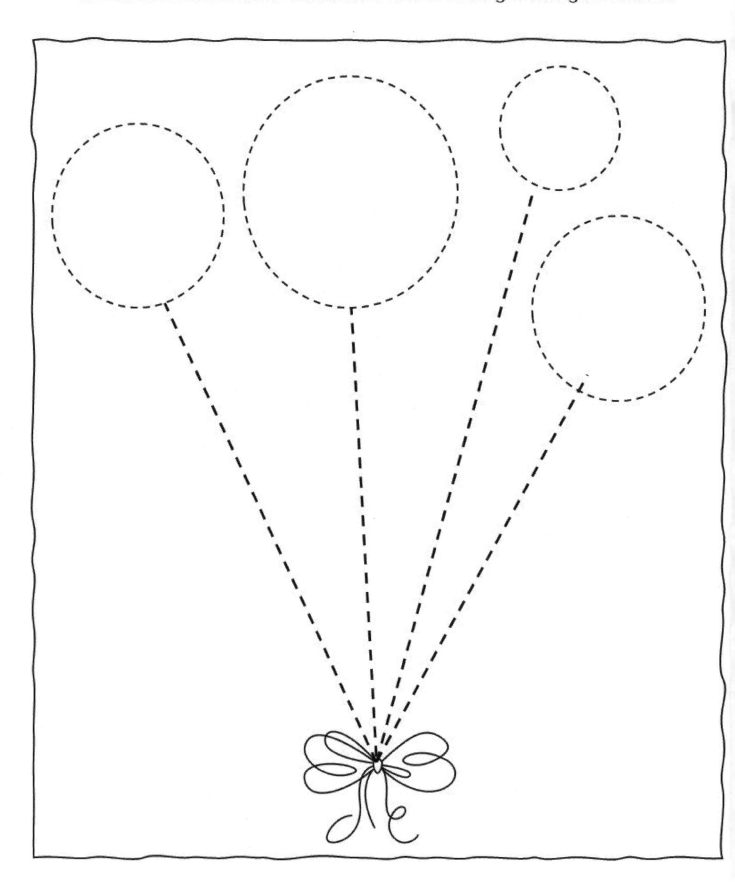

Writing Warm-Up 3

Directions: Trace around the balloons and the strings leading to the bow.

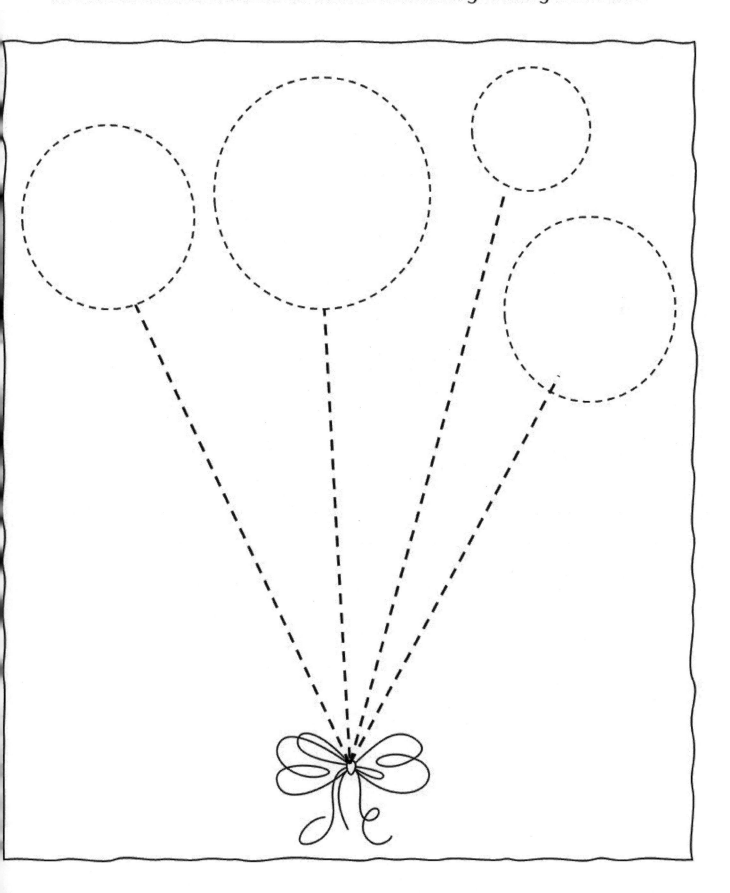

I Can Trace All My Letters

Directions: Trace the upper and lower case letters on each line.

I Can Trace All My Letters

Directions: Trace the upper and lower case letters on each line.

I Can Trace All My Letters

Directions: Trace the upper and lower case letters on each line.

I Can Trace All My Letters

Directions: Trace the upper and lower case letters on each line.

I Can Trace All My Letters

Directions: Trace the upper and lower case letters on each line.

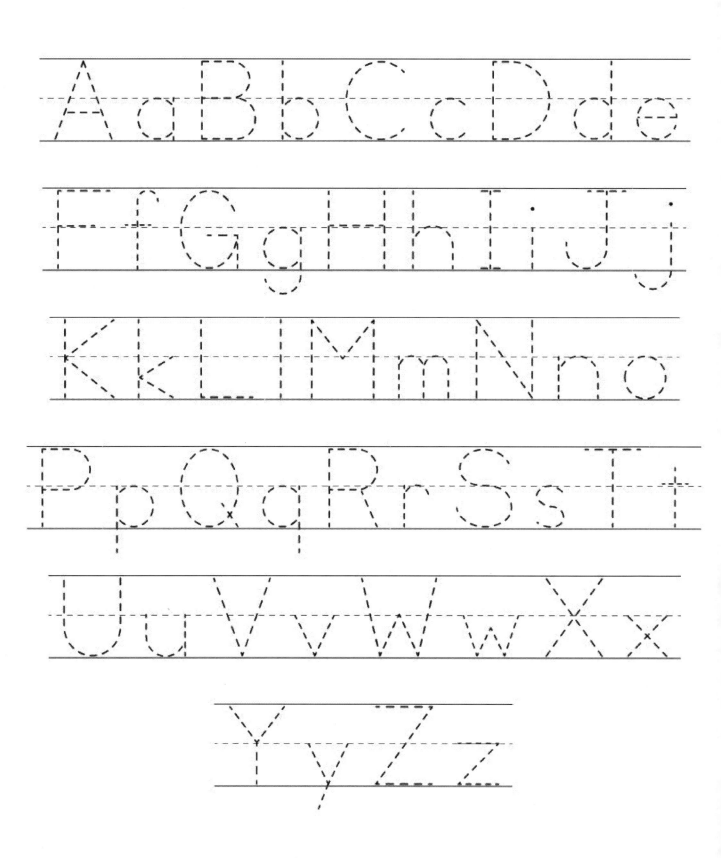

I Can Trace All My Letters

Directions: Trace the upper and lower case letters on each line.

I Can Find the Letters in My Name #1

Directions: Find the letters in your name and color them.

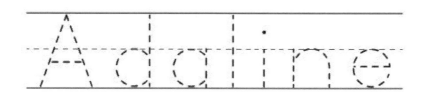

	A	B	C
D	E	F	G
H	I	J	K
L	M	N	O
P	Q	R	S
T	U	V	W
X	Y	Z	

I Can Find the Letters in My Name #2

Directions: Find the letters in your name and color them.

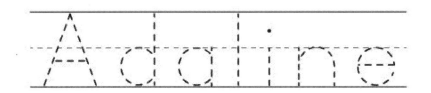

	a	b	c
d	e	f	g
h	i	j	k
l	m	n	o
p	q	r	s
t	u	v	w
x	y	z	

My Name Is

Directions: Color the letters of your name.

ADALINE

And This Is Me

Directions: Draw a picture of yourself.

I Can Color this Narwhal and My Name

Directions: Write your name on the white part of the card and then decorate it.

All About My Name

Directions: Trace your name and write your answer.

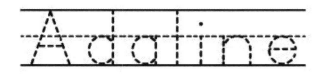

My name starts
with a

My name ends
with a

My name has this
many letters

Directions: Circle the letters in your name.

A B C D E F G

H I J K L M N O

P Q R S T U V

W X Y Z

I'm Ready to Start Writing My Name

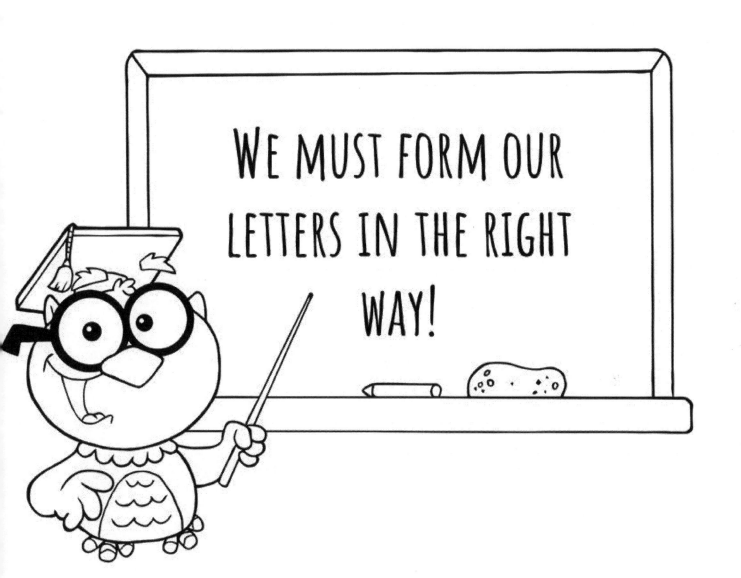

WE MUST FORM OUR LETTERS IN THE RIGHT WAY!

This Is How I Make My Letters

Directions: Follow and trace the lines in for each letter.

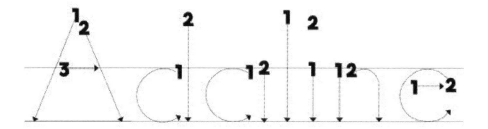

Directions: Let's practice some more.

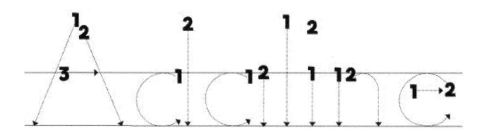

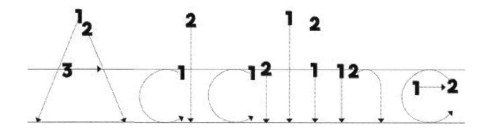

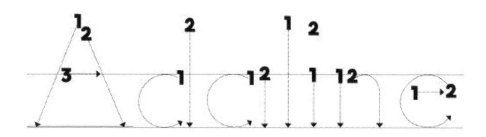

This Is How I Make My Letters

Directions: Follow and trace the lines in for each letter.

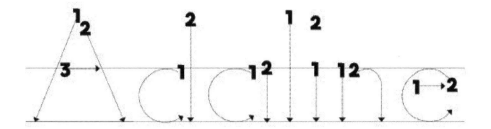

Directions: Let's practice some more.

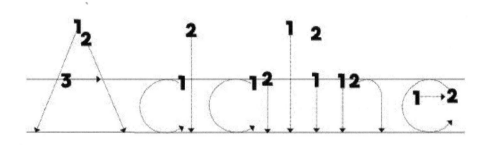

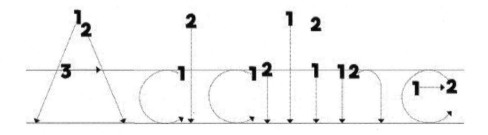

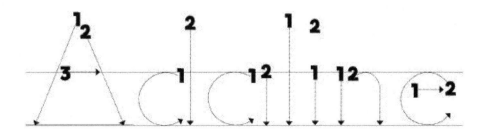

This Is How I Make My Letters

Directions: Follow and trace the lines in for each letter.

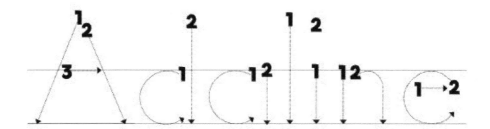

Directions: Let's practice some more.

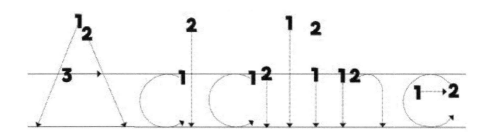

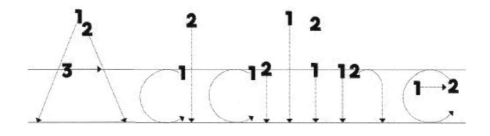

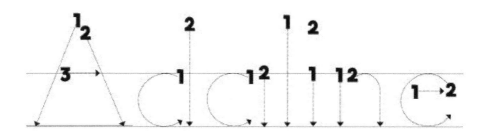

This Is How I Make My Letters

Directions: Follow and trace the lines in for each letter.

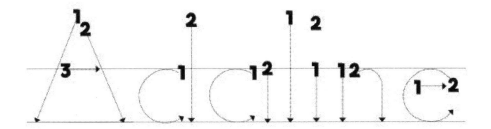

Directions: Let's practice some more.

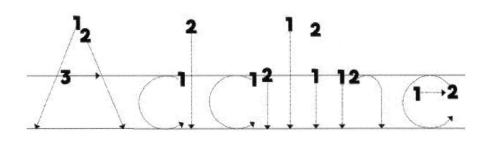

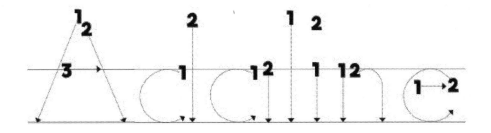

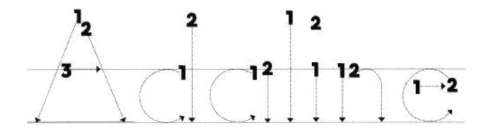

This Is How I Make My Letters

Directions: Follow and trace the lines in for each letter.

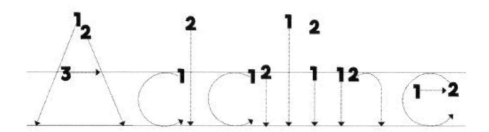

Directions: Let's practice some more.

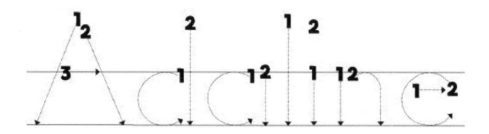

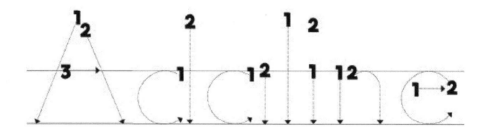

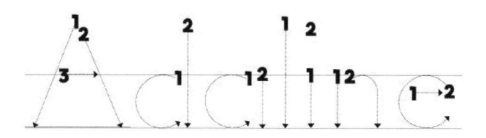

This Is How I Make My Letters

Directions: Follow and trace the lines in for each letter.

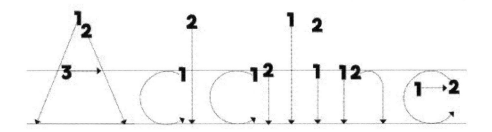

Directions: Let's practice some more.

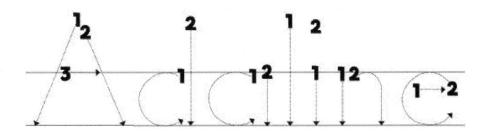

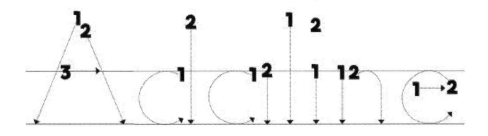

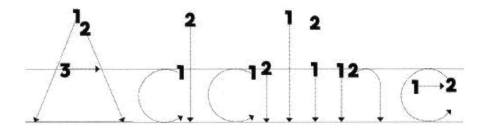

I Can Dot Touch and Write My Name

Directions: Touch the dots as you spell you name then trace it at the bottom.

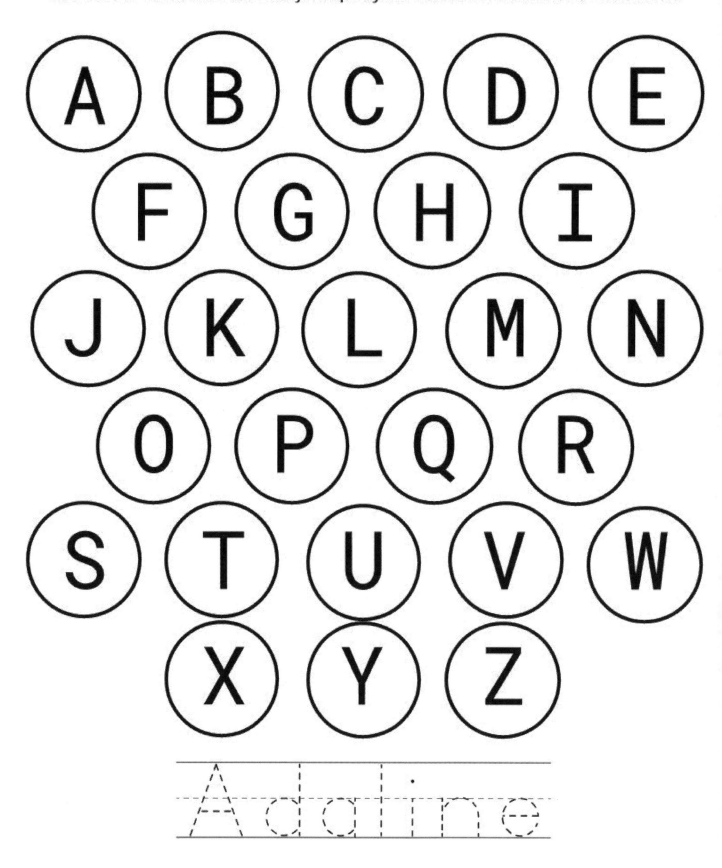

I Can Dot Touch and Write My Name

Directions: Touch the dots as you spell you name then trace it at the bottom.

I Can Dot Touch and Write My Name

Directions: Touch the dots as you spell you name then trace it at the bottom.

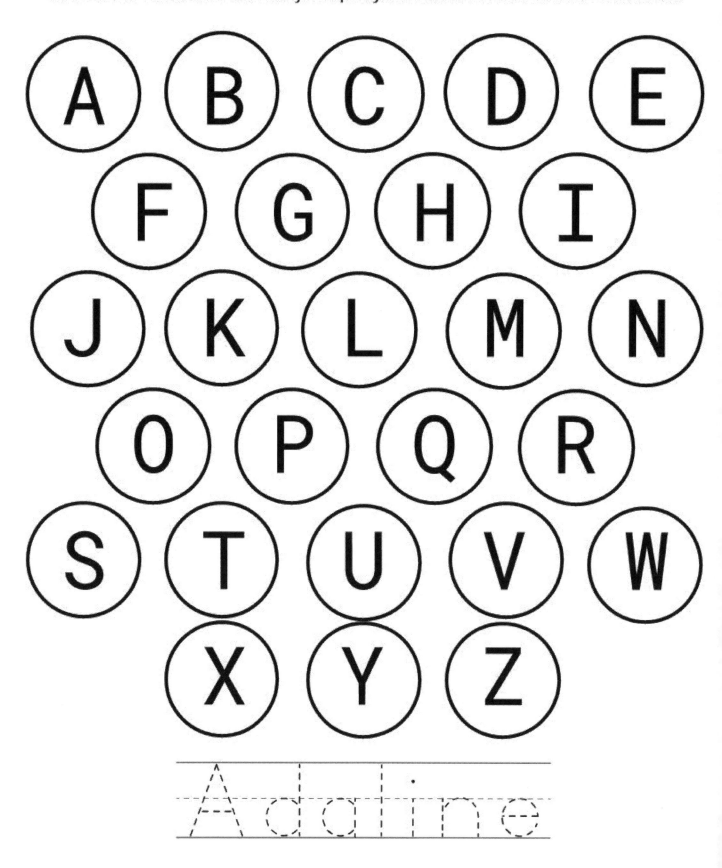

I Can Dot Touch and Write My Name

Directions: Touch the dots as you spell you name then trace it at the bottom.

This Is How Color My Name

Directions: Color your name in blue.

Adaline

Directions: Color your name in yellow.

Directions: Color your name in red.

Directions: Color your name in green.

ADALINE

I'm a Tracing Ace

Directions: Trace your name and color the kids and sign.

Great

Job!

Adaline

This Is How I Trace My Name

Directions: Follow and trace your name.

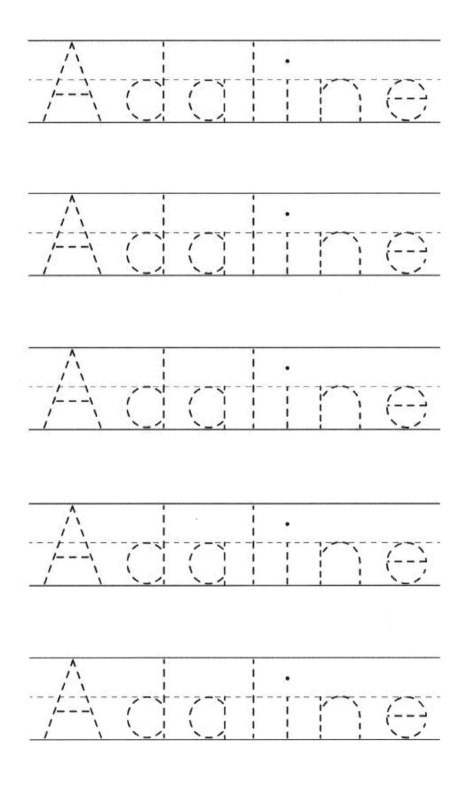

This Is How I Trace My Name

Directions: Follow and trace your name.

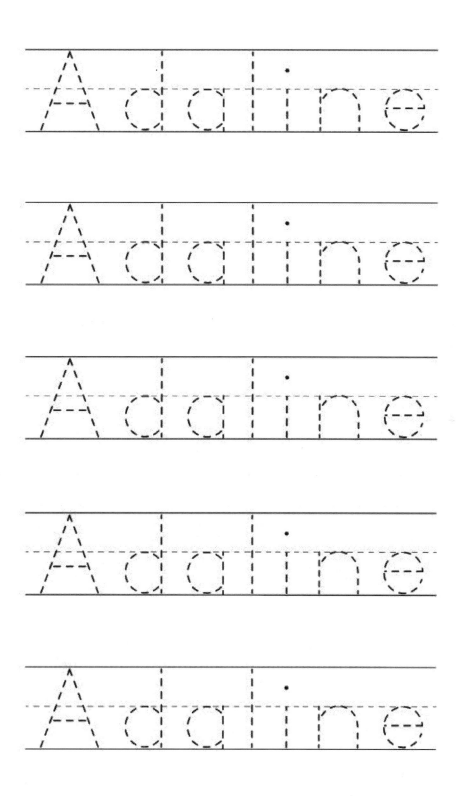

This Is How I Trace My Name

Directions: Follow and trace your name.

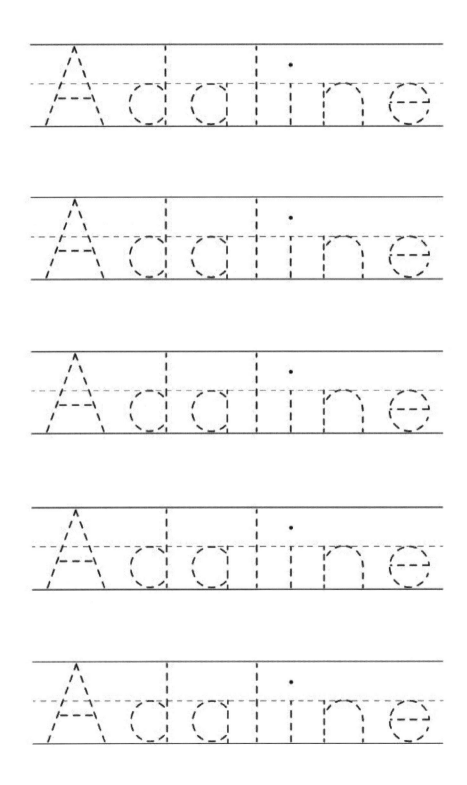

This Is How I Trace My Name

Directions: Follow and trace your name.

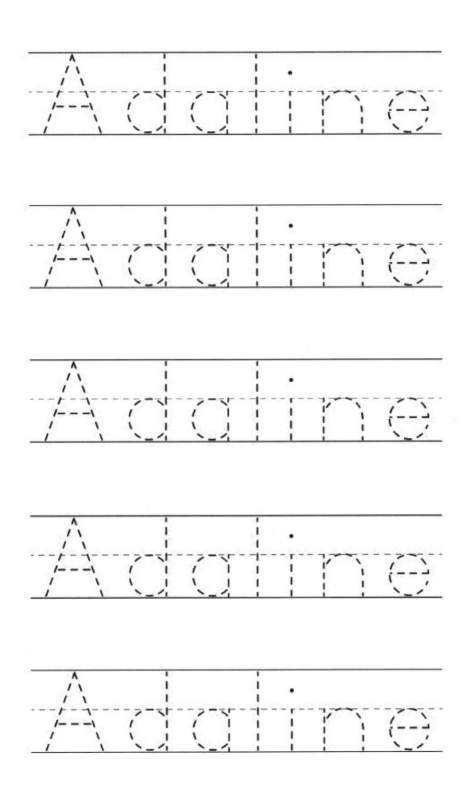

This Is How I Trace My Name

Directions: Follow and trace your name.

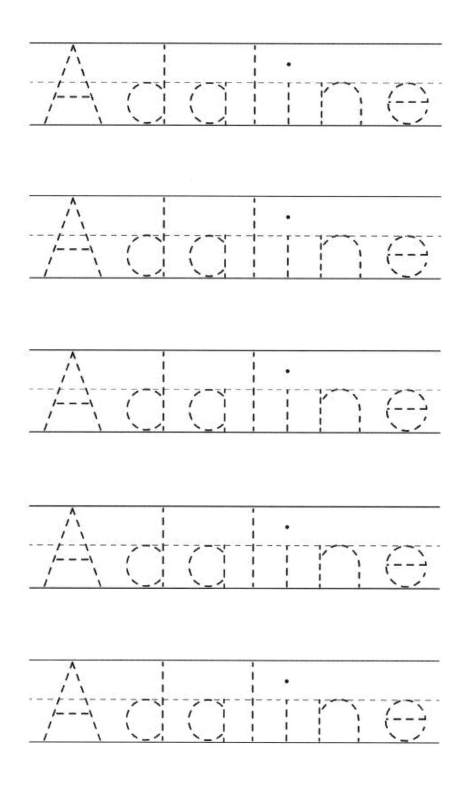

This Is How I Trace My Name

Directions: Follow and trace your name.

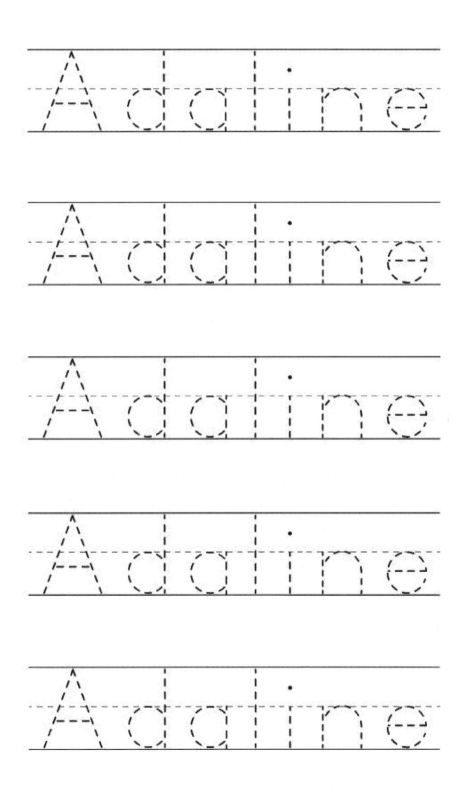

This Is How I Trace My Name

Directions: Follow and trace your name.

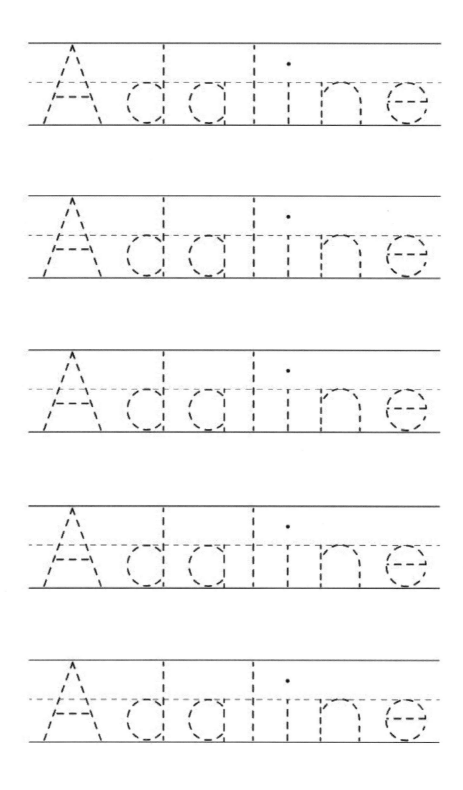

This Is How I Trace My Name

Directions: Follow and trace your name.

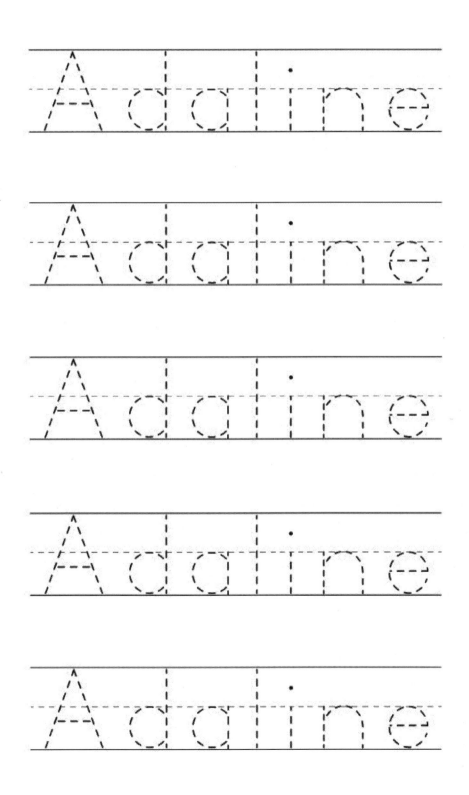

This Is How I Trace My Name

Directions: Follow and trace your name.

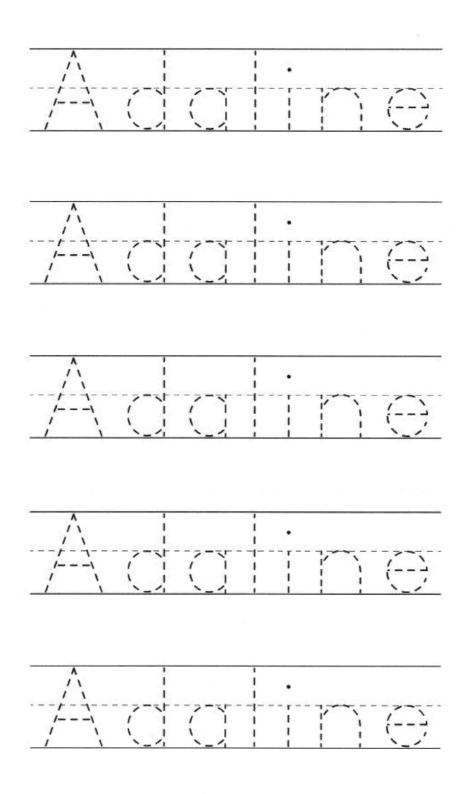

This Is How I Trace My Name

Directions: Follow and trace your name.

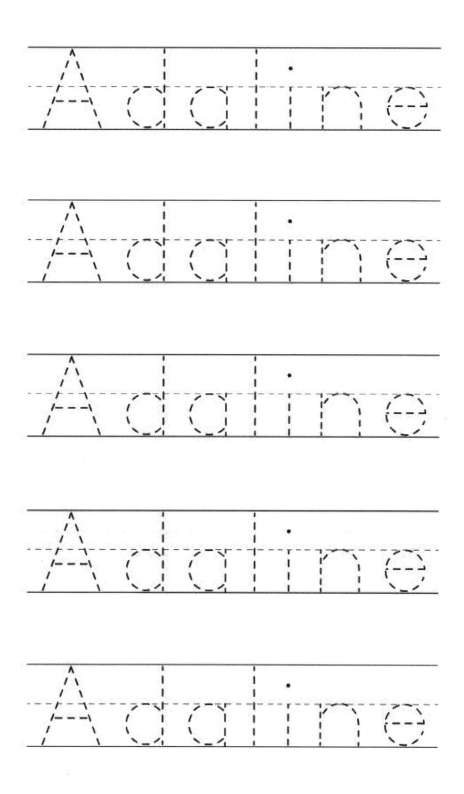

This Is How I Trace My Name

Directions: Follow and trace your name.

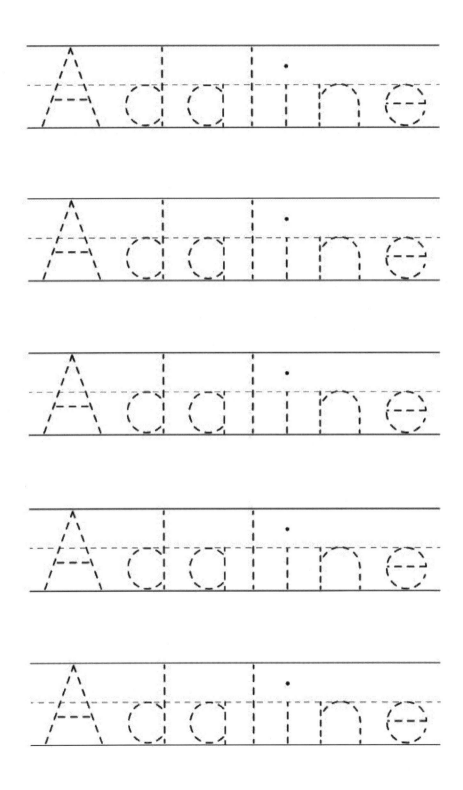

This Is How I Trace My Name

Directions: Follow and trace your name.

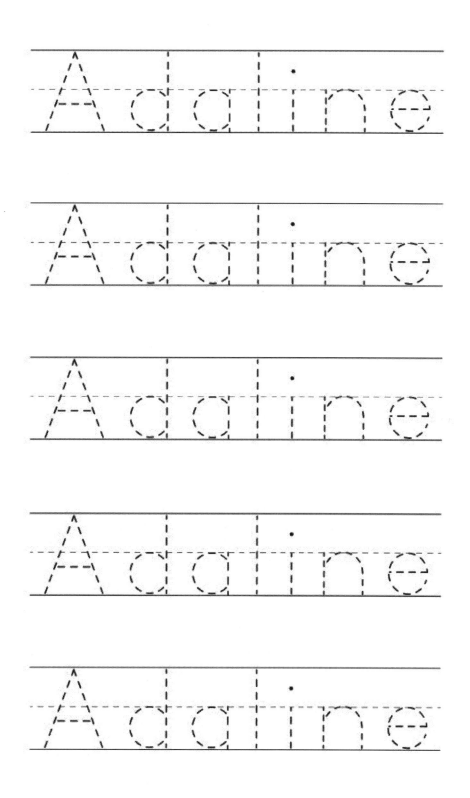

This Is How I Trace My Name

Directions: Follow and trace your name.

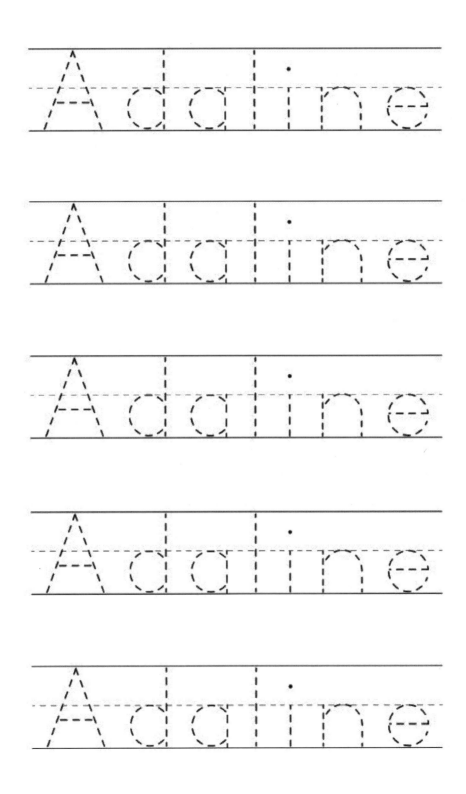

This Is How I Trace My Name

Directions: Follow and trace your name.

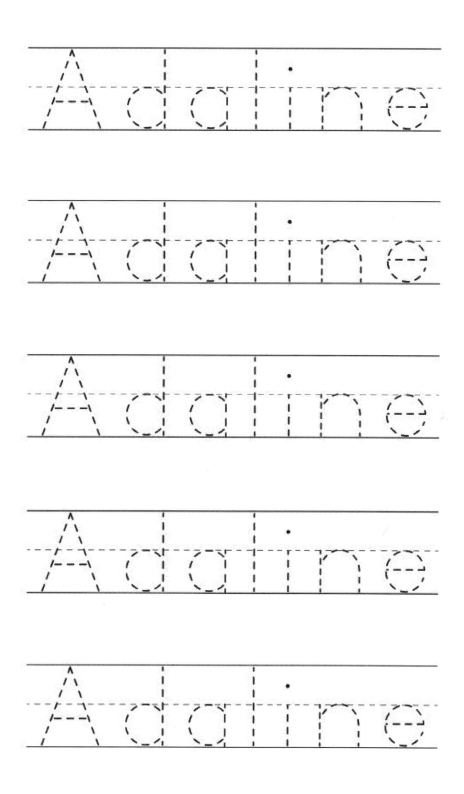

This Is How I Trace My Name

Directions: Follow and trace your name.

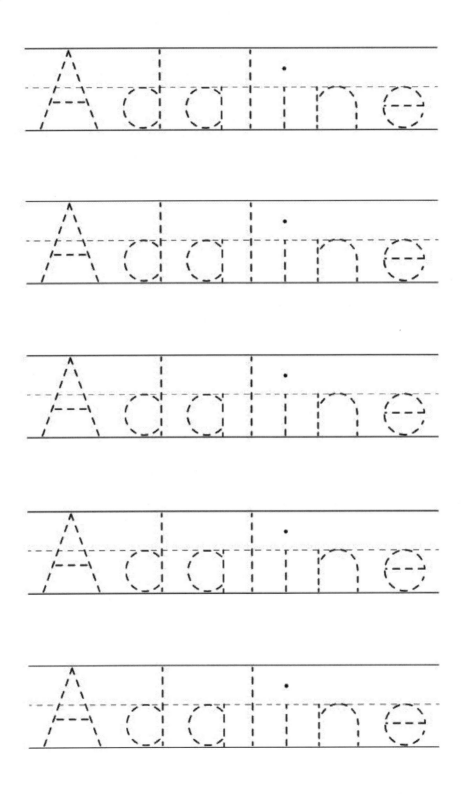

This Is How I Trace My Name

Directions: Follow and trace your name.

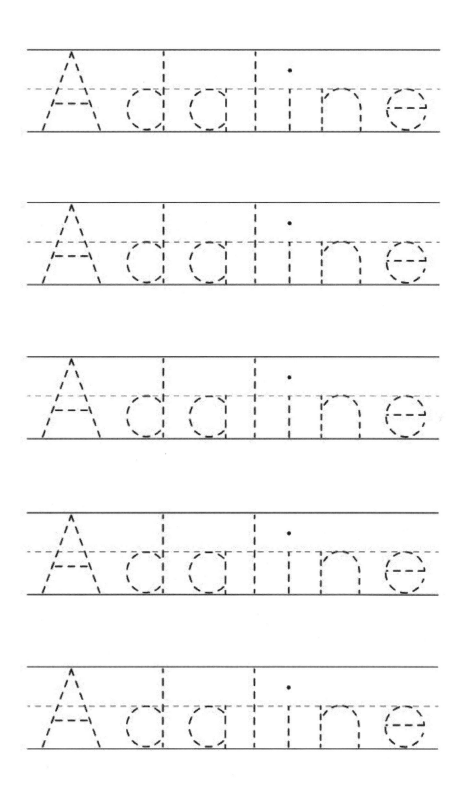

This Is How I Trace My Name

Directions: Follow and trace your name.

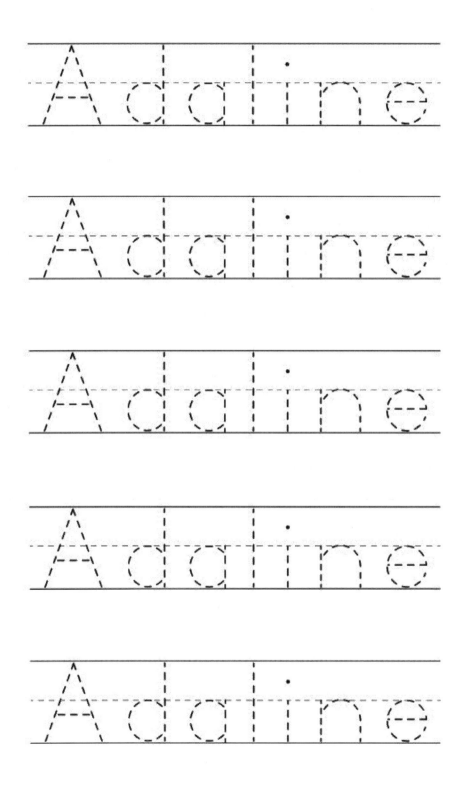

This Is How I Trace My Name

Directions: Follow and trace your name.

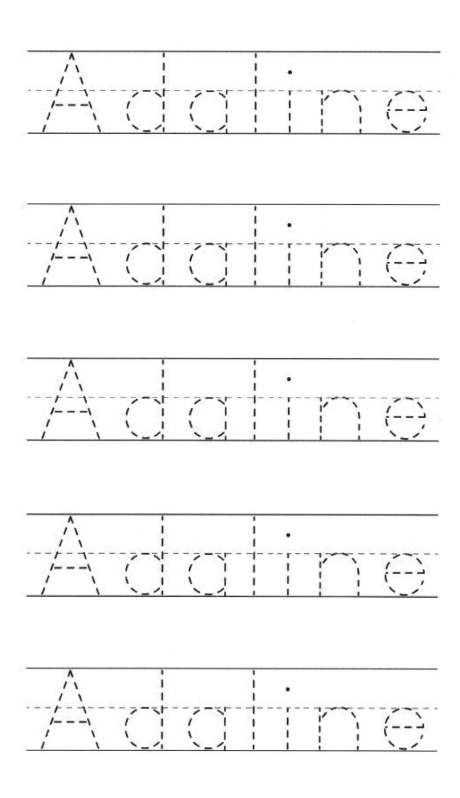

This Is How I Trace My Name

Directions: Follow and trace your name.

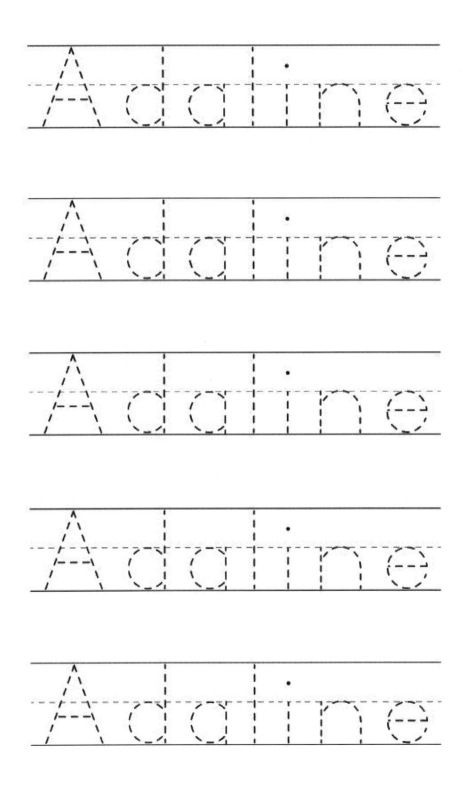

This Is How I Trace My Name

Directions: Follow and trace your name.

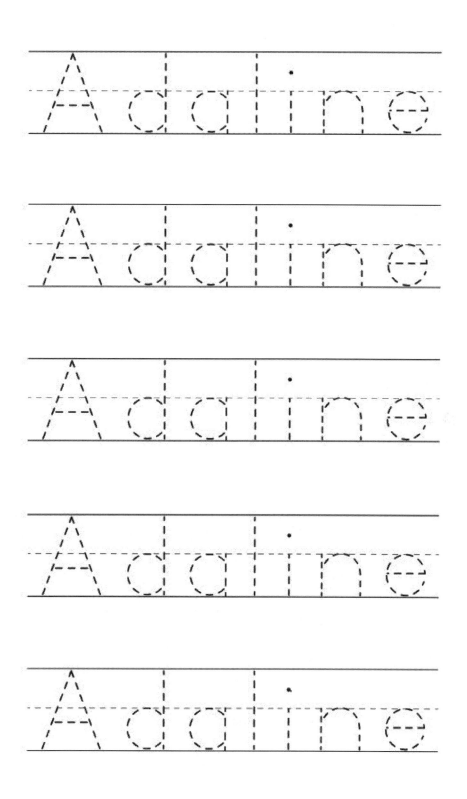

I Can Spell, Trace and Find My Name

Directions: Point to each letter in your name and say it out loud.

Directions: Trace and say each letter of you name.

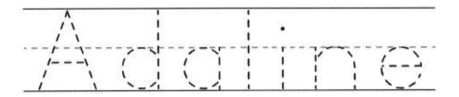

Directions: Now, just trace your name.

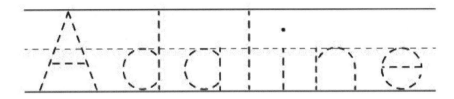

Directions: Find the letters that make your name. Circle in another color if the letter/letters are used more than once).

Yeah, You're doing so good, Adaline.

Now let's practice writing your name.

This Is How I Write My Name

Directions: Trace your name and then write it yourself.

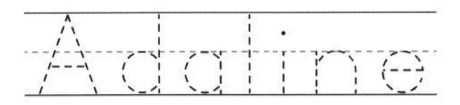

This Is How I Write My Name

Directions: Trace your name and then write it yourself.

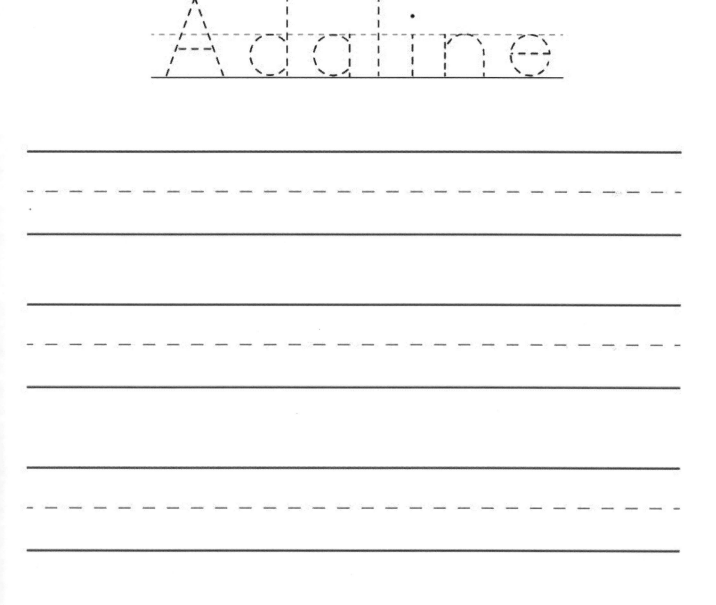

This Is How I Write My Name

Directions: Trace your name and then write it yourself.

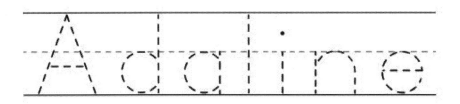

This Is How I Write My Name

Directions: Trace your name and then write it yourself.

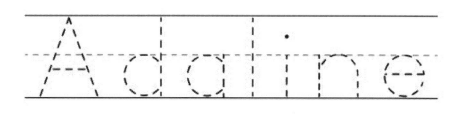

This Is How I Write My Name

Directions: Trace your name and then write it yourself.

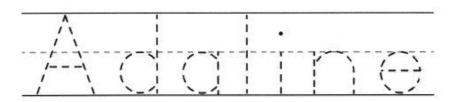

This Is How I Write My Name

Directions: Trace your name and then write it yourself.

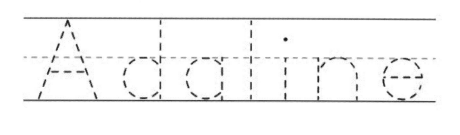

This Is How I Write My Name

Directions: Trace your name and then write it yourself.

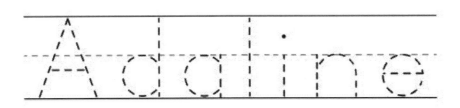

This Is How I Write My Name

Directions: Trace your name and then write it yourself.

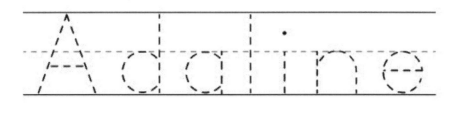

I Can Write My Name By Myself

Directions: Write your name on the line below and color in the be.

Adaline

Show me how you write your name.

- -

This Is How I Write My Name

Directions: Now, write your name by yourself.

This Is How I Write My Name

Directions: Now, write your name by yourself.

This Is How I Write My Name

Directions: Now, write your name by yourself.

This Is How I Write My Name

Directions: Now, write your name by yourself.

This Is How I Write My Name

Directions: Now, write your name by yourself.

This Is How I Write My Name

Directions: Now, write your name by yourself.

This Is How I Write My Name

Directions: Now, write your name by yourself.

This Is How I Write My Name

Directions: Now, write your name by yourself.

This Is How I Write My Name

Directions: Now, write your name by yourself.

This Is How I Write My Name

Directions: Now, write your name by yourself.

This Is How I Write My Name

Directions: Now, write your name by yourself.

This Is How I Write My Name

Directions: Now, write your name by yourself.

This Is How I Write My Name

Directions: Now, write your name by yourself.

I'm One Smart Cookie Because I Can Write My Name

Directions: Write your name on the line below and color in the cookie.

This Is How I Write My Name
in a Box (without lines)

Directions: Follow and trace your name.

This Is How I Write My Name
in a Box (without lines)

Directions: Follow and trace your name.

This Is How I Write My Name in a Box (without lines)

Directions: Follow and trace your name.

This Is How I Write My Name
in a Box (without lines)

Directions: Follow and trace your name.

This Is How I Write My Name
in a Box (without lines)

Directions: Follow and trace your name.

This Is How I Write My Name
in a Box (without lines)

Directions: Follow and trace your name.

This Is How I Write My Name in a Box (without lines)

Directions: Follow and trace your name.

This Is How I Write My Name in a Box (without lines)

Directions: Follow and trace your name.

This Is How I Write My Name
in a Box (without lines)

Directions: Follow and trace your name.

This Is How I Write My Name in a Box (without lines)

Directions: Follow and trace your name.

This Is How I Write My Name in a Box (without lines)

Directions: Follow and trace your name.

This Is How I Write My Name
in a Box (without lines)

Directions: Follow and trace your name.

This Is How I Write My Name in a Box (without lines)

Directions: Follow and trace your name.

I Can Find My Name

Directions: Find your name in these names and circle it, then trace it on the line.

ANDREW   SAMUEL   BAILEY   AVA

ISABELLA   AUDREY   JACK   BROOKE

HARPER   AARON   MIGUEL

CHLOE   ADALINE   MACKENZIE

JAYDEN   THEODORE   EMMA   TY

LILLIAN   MADELYN   GREYSON   IVY

ANGEL   MASON   JACKSON

- -

I Can Make a Placecard with My Name

Directions: Write your name on the white part of the card and then decorate it.

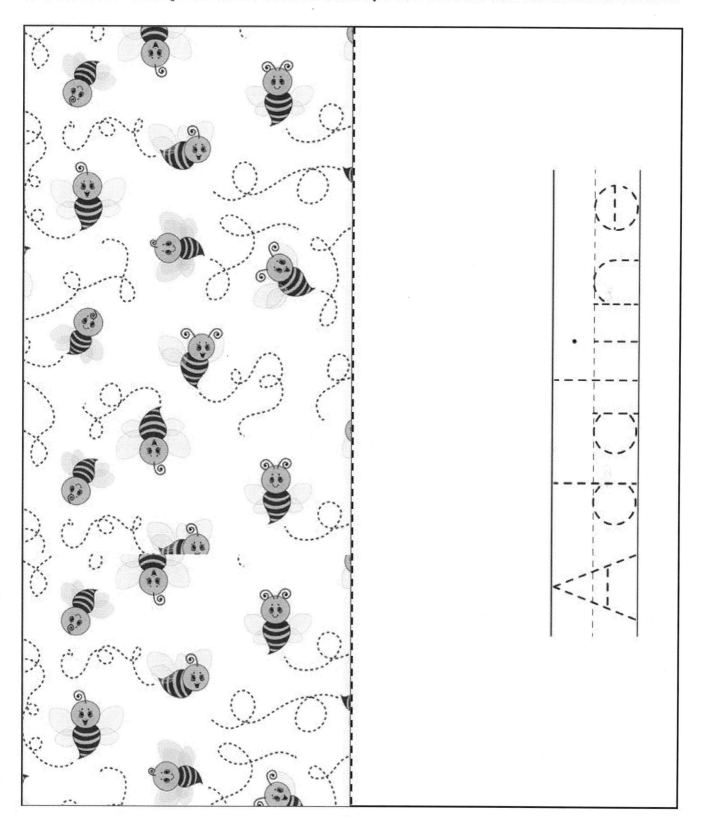

Directions: Cute out the placecard, fold on the dotted line and place on your desk.

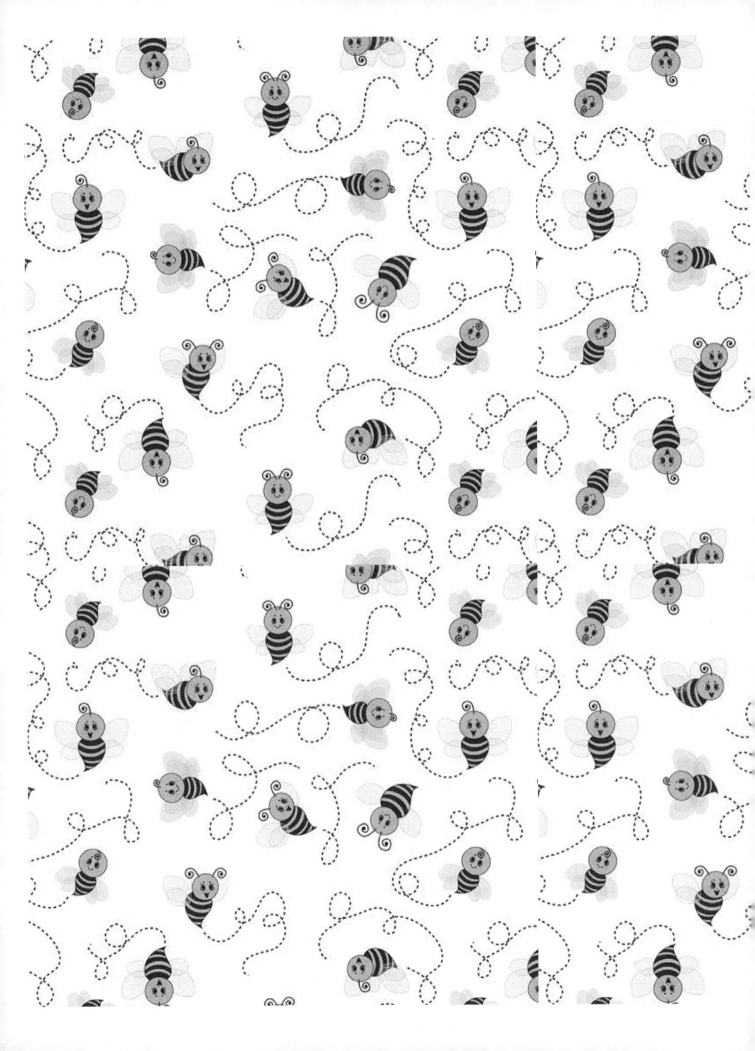